The S(
DECLARATION
of
INDEPENDENCE

PUBLISHER
ARTISAN PUBLISHERS
P.O. Box 1529
Muskogee, Oklahoma 74402
(918) 682-8341
www.artisanpublishers.com

NORTH

WEST

CENTRAL HIGHLANDS

●INVERNESS

●GRANTOWN

NORTH EAST

●AVIEMORE

HIGHLANDS

●FORT WILLIAM

●PITLOCHRY

CENTRAL SCOTLAND

OBAN●

GLASGOW●

●EDINBURGH

LOTHIANS and BORDERS

CLYDE COAST and SOUTH WEST

AYR●

●DUMFRIES

STRANRAER●

●KIRKCUDBRIGHT

MAP OF MODERN SCOTLAND

2

INTRODUCTION

"Scotland's most precious possession" is what many call the letter from King Robert (the Bruce) of Scotland to Pope John XXII. Known today as the "Declaration of Arbroath" or "The Scottish Declaration of Independence" it may be seen in a shallow glass case in the Register House of Edinburgh. The document is a parchment to which are attached twenty-five red and green seals — the seals of the subscribing Scottish nobles.

Bruce's letter preserves an intriguing allusion to the origin of the Scots and provides one link to the solution of one of history's most fascinating problems. What was the fate of the so-called "Ten Lost Tribes of Israel?" The Declaration not only contains a record of the origin of the Scottish people, but indicates the route of their previous migrations.

The Declaration's authority rests not on a single individual (King Robert Bruce) but is attested by the signature of twenty-five Scottish nobles. It was drawn up by Bernard de Linton, Abbot of Aberbrothick and Chancellor of Scotland, and was sent to Pope John XXII by the Scottish Estates in the Parliament assembled in the Abbey of Aberbrothick under the Presidence of King Robert the Bruce, and is dated the 6th of April, A.D. 1320.

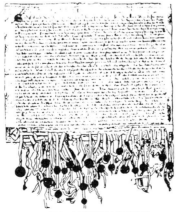

THE DECLARATION OF ARBROATH

3

ROBERT THE BRUCE (1274-1329)

SCOTLAND THE BRAVE

Hark when the night is falling,
Hear, hear the pipes are calling,
Loudly and proudly calling
Down through the glen.
There where the hills are sleeping,
Now feel the blood a-leaping,
High as the spirits of the old Highland men.

    Towering in gallant fame,
    Scotland, my mountain hame [home],
    High may your proud standards gloriously
      wave.
    Land of my high endeavour,
    Land of the shining river,
    Land of my heart for ever,
    Scotland the Brave.

ROBERT BRUCE

Scotland's greatest patriot king was descended from a Norman knight, Sir Robert de Brus who came to England with William the Conqueror. When David I of Scotland gave his childhood friend, Robert de Brus, (1141 A.D.) a grant of Annandale, the family put down their first territorial roots in Scotland. Robert, the future king, was born June 11, 1274 in Turnberry Castle, Ayr. Robert's father (6th Lord of Annandale) became 1st Earl of Carrick (by marriage) and with other nobility, formed the "communitas regni Scotie" (community of the realm of Scotland). Under feudal law, these nobles were obliged to perform military service for their king — when they had one.

In 1286 King Alexander III of Scotland, nightriding on his way from Edinburgh to Kinghorn to join his newly-acquired second wife (Yolette de Dreux), fell to his death over a cliff. His unexpected death left the infant daughter (Margaret) of the King of Norway, as successor to the throne. His first wife, Margaret, both his sons and his daughter, the Queen of Norway, had died a year before him. Yolette de Dreux, whom he had married the year before his death had as yet borne him no children.

As the infant Queen (the Maid of Norway) was still in Norway, six Guardians were appointed as collective caretakers of the Scottish kingdom. England's King Edward I, a shrewd, ruthless man, who had been king since 1272, came forward with the proposal that Margaret should marry his six year old son, Edward. This would unite the four island kingdoms under his crown. Margaret, at this time was seven years of age. The caretakers agreed to this proposal and the marriage was arranged.

The Treaty of Birgham (1290) that contained the marriage agreement, also stipulated that Scotland was to remain "separate and divided from the kingdom of England." However, Edward I had other ideas in mind that

BUTTRESS STATUES OF EDWARD I AND HIS QUEEN,
ELEANOR OF CASTILE, AT LINCOLN CATHEDRAL

6

time would reveal. But, before the marriage could be formally legalized, Margaret perished on Orkney on her voyage from Norway to England. Thirteen competitors laid claim to her vacant throne. The two frontrunners, both descended from David I's son, Henry of Northumberland, were: the future King Robert's grandfather, Robert Bruce, 5th Lord of Annandale and John Balliol, Lord of Galloway.

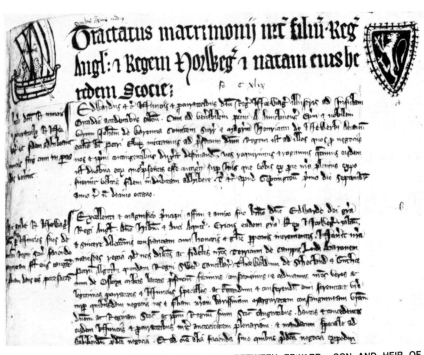

PROPOSED TREATY OF MARRIAGE DATED 1290 BETWEEN EDWARD, SON AND HEIR OF EDWARD I OF ENGLAND AND MARARITE OF NORWAY.

The Guardians of Scotland, who couldn't decide which claimant should receive the crown, unwisely asked Edward I of England to make the choice. Edward I took advantage of the Scottish political crisis to announce (at the Anglo-Scottish Parliament of Norham — 1291) that he had come in his capacity as "superior and lord paramount of the kingdom of Scotland" and must be formally acknowledged as such, before any choice could be made.

Rebuffed by the Guardians, Edward I persuaded seven

7

SEAL OF BALLIOL SHOWING HIM SEATED ON THE THRONE

SEAL OF JOHN BALLIOL. SHOWING AS A MOUNTED WARRIOR

8

of the competitors to acknowledge him as their feudal superior and overlord of Scotland. Competitors Robert Bruce and John Balliol both accepted Edward I's terms. However, Bruce, realizing his advanced age might give Balliol an advantage over him, transferred his royal claim to his son, Robert (Nov. 7, 1291). He, in turn, passed the Earldom of Carrick to his 18 year-old son Robert, the future king. This action made little difference to Edward I, who decided in favor of John Balliol. After duly acknowledging Edward I as his overlord, Balliol received a traditional coronation at Scone to begin a three-year reign of continued appeasement and humiliation by the English king.

WARRANT OF EDWARD I AS OVERLORD OF SCOTLAND (JULY 4, 1292)

When Edward returned to London he took with him much of the royal plate and jewelry and the ancient Crowning Stone (the Lia Fail) of the Scottish kings which Fergus the Great of Dalriada had brought from Ireland seven centuries earlier. Edward then had the Stone encased in a Chair fashioned by Master Walter of Durham, the king's

9

THE CORONATION THRONE

painter, for one hundred crowns. Today, the Stone can be seen in Westminster Abbey beneath the chair known as the Coronation Throne.

The Coronation Stone, through the evidence of legend, history and tradition point to the origin of the Stone as that which the Hebrew patriarch, Jacob (re-named Israel) annointed with oil at Bethel three and a half thousand years ago. Although the regalia of Scotland was returned to Scotland by Edward III, the Coronation Stone only once left the Abbey since 1297. It was last used in the Coronation Service of Her Majesty, Queen Elizabeth the Second on June 2, 1953.

EDWARD I, 1272-1307

When Edward I declared war against Philip IV of France (June 24, 1294) and demanded military service from his vassals in Wales and Scotland, a resistance movement, led by twelve Scottish nobles, persuaded Balliol to defy the English king. The Bruce family, however, had no inclination to serve Balliol's interests. So, when the competitor Bruce died (in 1295) his son and grandson remained loyal to Edward I, on whose side they were ranged as the wars of independence began. For this they were dispossessed of their lands by Balliol.

The Bruce families' choice of loyalty to the English king proved to be a wise one. In response to Balliol's resistance, Edward I invaded Scotland in 1296, capturing Berwick, Dunbar and Brechin. At Brechin, Edward I then summoned 2,000 Scottish nobles to Berwick castle and demanded, as a price for peace, they put their seals to the Ragman Rolls, as

11

recognition of his control over their kingdom. The loyalty of Robert Bruce (2nd Earl of Carrick) to Edward I was rewarded by the restoration of the Earldom Balliol had confiscated.

THE RAYMAN ROLLS

Out of this moment of national humiliation, a Scottish champion emerged — William Wallace of Elderslie, Renfrewshire. Wallace became involved in a brawl with some English soldiers in the market place at Lanark. He managed to escape arrest with the help of a girl who some say was his wife. The girl, however, was caught and put to death by the Sheriff of Lanark. Wallace was distressed by the Sheriff's action and that night he killed the Sheriff and became an outlaw.

Wallace's anti-English feelings turned into an organized revolt. With a band of desperate men that had been outlawed by the English, he continued the struggle for Scottish independence. He successfully led various attacks on English strongholds, each success bringing more men under his command. In a short time Wallace recovered almost all of the fortresses held by the English. Robert Bruce decided to join the Scottish rebels while his father, Lord of Annandale, maintained his support of the English. Bruce, himself, explained his political conversion in these words: "I must join my own people and the nation in which I was born." Little did Robert know he was destined to play an important role in the Scottish fight for independence.

Hearing that an English army (led by the Earl of Surrey) was marching northward, Wallace made a rapid march to Stirling in time to engage the English as they attempted to cross the bridge over the passage of the Forth. When about half of the English army had crossed the bridge, Wallace's men attacked with such fury that the English fled in all directions, in complete disorder. Many were slain by the sword or driven into the river to drown. Those on the south side of the river were seized with panic and fled tumultuously, having first set fire to the bridge. The Scots, however, crossed by a ford and continued the pursuit of the English as far south as Berwick.

The results of the English defeat at Stirling caused the English to retreat everywhere from Scotland. To increase the alarm of the English, as well as to relieve the famine which then prevailed, Wallace organized a great raid into the northern parts of England. After devastating the country as far as the gates of Newcastle, Wallace returned to Scotland and was elected (or assumed) the title of Guardian of Scotland. While in this office, he set himself to reorganize the army and to regulate the affairs of his country. His measures were marked by wisdom and vigor and for a short time succeeded in securing order, even in the face of jealousy and opposition from many of the nobles.

Edward I was in Flanders when the news of this successful revolt reached him. He hastened home, and at the head of a great army entered Scotland in July 1298. Wallace slowly retreated before the English monarch, driving off all supplies and wasting the countryside. The Scottish nobles as usual, for the most part, deserted his standard. Meanwhile,

Edward I, compelled by famine, gave orders for the English army to retreat. However, before his orders could be carried out, news was received concerning desertions from Wallace's army as they retreated northward. Armed with this information, Edward I issued new orders for his soldiers to march against the Scots with all haste.

When the English army, then at Kirkliston, received their new orders, they hurried north and engaged the Scottish army (at Falkirk) the morning of July 22, 1298. After an obstinate fight, the Scots were overpowered and defeated with great loss of life. Wallace escaped capture and as he fled north with a remnant of his army, burned the town and castle of Stirling on his way. Wallace then resigned the office of Guardian of Scotland, but pursued predatory warfare against the English. He is known to have made one trip to France with the purpose of obtaining aid for his country from the French king. During this period in history, Robert Bruce appeared to support Edward I, but secretly sided with his countrymen. He is known to have entered into a bond of support for the Scottish cause with William Lamberton, Bishop of St. Andrews. Lamberton and Robert had been appointed by Edward I, as co-regents of Scotland in 1299 A.D.

With Wallace in hiding, the fight for an independent Scotland seemed futile. So, if the end-product was simply to be the triumph of the Balliol family interests at the expense of his own, Robert decided to submit to the English. In return for his services, Edward I guaranteed "life and limb, lands and tenements" and granted a pardon (1302 A.D.) As if to cement his new bond with the English, Robert married Elizabeth de Burgh, daughter of Edward I's follower, the Earl of Ulster. This was Robert's second marriage. His first marriage was to Isabella, daughter of Donald, Earl of Mar. This union produced a daughter, Marjory, who in turn produced the first Stuart king.

In the meantime, Edward I was eliminating all pockets of resistance. In the winter of 1303-1304 A.D., Edward I asked for and received the submission of most of the Scottish nobles. Wallace was expressly excepted from all terms and a price was set upon his head. The English officials in Scotland were given orders to use every means to effect his capture. On August 5, 1305, Wallace was captured near Glasgow, through treachery it is alleged, and conveyed to London in chains. He reached London on the 22nd of August and the next day was taken to Westminster Hall where he was impeached as a traitor by Sir Peter Mallorie.

To the accusation of treason, Wallace made the simple reply that he could not be a traitor to the King of England, for he had never been a subject and never swore fealty to him. His defense was ignored and Wallace was found guilty and condemned to death. On August 24th he was hung, drawn and quartered and beheaded. To discourage the others, Edward I had Wallace's piked head displayed on London Bridge while the four parts of his mutilated body were sent to Newcastle, Berwick, Stirling and Perth. The Scottish poet, Blind Harry, ends his epic about Wallace as follows:

"Scotland he freed, brought it off bondage.
And now in Heaven he had his heritage."

After the unusually savage execution of Wallace, Edward I sought to conciliate the Scottish nobles by granting a liberal constitution to Scotland. Robert Bruce is reputed to have been one of the advisors of such action. But, when it became apparent his fidelity to King Edward I was

ALTHOUGH WALLACE HAS NO STATELY MONUMENT, HE LIVES ON IN THE HEROIC HISTORY OF SCOTLAND. HE LOST THE BATTLE FOR SCOTLAND'S FREEDOM, BUT HE STARTED THE CAMPAIGN WHICH WAS TO WIN IT.

suspected, Robert secretly returned to Scotland. There, embittered by the manner of Wallace's death and stirred by patriotic zeal for his country, Robert surreptitiously organized resistance to the English while gaining support for his own right to the Scottish crown.

Unbeknown to Robert, one of his countrymen, John Comyn (a nephew of Balliol) was a traitor who was in direct touch with the English king and faithfully relayed the plans of the plotters as fast as they were made. Robert knew that "Red" John Comyn of Badenoch, was an obstacle that had to be cleared from his path to the Scottish throne. If Comyn would not be an ally, then he was much too formidable to be tolerated as an enemy. His pedigree was impeccable and he had many friends, including some English, in high places. So, on February 10, 1306, Robert met with Comyn in the Franciscan church of Greyfriars in Dumfries Abbey.

Standing in front of the high altar of the church, the two men discussed politics and rebellion until it became apparent to Robert that Comyn had no intention of supporting his claim to the Scottish crown. So uncompromisingly fierce was Comyn's rejection of Robert's offer of his lands in return for help in restoring an independent Scottish monarchy under Robert that Robert drew his dagger and stabbed the Lord of Badenoch. Robert's followers finished off Comyn and also struck down Sir Robert Comyn when he came forward to defend his wounded nephew. (Some authorities state that Robert was aware of Comyn's treachery and followed him into the Abbey for the purpose of killing him).

Knowing his plans could no longer be kept from the English king, Robert promptly gathered his adherents and marched to Scone. There, in the presence of only five earls, four bishops and one abbot — and with the ill-omened absence of the crowning stone (Stone of Scone) Robert Bruce received the Scottish crown (March 26, 1306) at the hands of a woman. This was the Countess of Buchan, who performed

GREAT SEAL OF ROBERT BRUCE, ON WHICH HE IS STYLED 'REX SCOTTORUM'.
HE WAS CROWNED ON PALM SUNDAY, 1306.

THE OBVERSE OF A ROBERT I SILVER PENNY
SHOWING THE KING WITH SCEPTRE AND CROWN

18

the ceremony in the default of her brother, the Earl of Fife. Thus, six weeks after the "sacrilegious" murder of Comyn, Robert was, at least nominally, King of Scotland. But the odds against him keeping the kingdom were absolutely enormous: Edward I's army had a hold on the country; the outraged Papacy had set the church against Robert; and Comyn's kinsmen were seething with moral indignation.

In spite of the odds against him, Robert set out to win his kingdom. His first obstacle was to defend his cause against Aymer de Valence (Comyn's brother-in-law) who had been appointed by Edward I to deal with "King Hob" (a diminutive lacking the dignity of "Robert"). In a pitched battle at Methven, near Perth (June 19, 1306). Robert's forces were defeated. With a few remaining followers, Robert fled west where, in August, he was almost captured near Tyndrum by the MacDougalls of Dairy, who were Comyn's kinsmen. One clansman got near enough to grasp Robert's shoulder clasp-brooch. The fugitive king killed his assailant but had to leave his brooch in the dead man's grasp.

THE BROOCH OF LORNE

Fearing for the safety of his family. Robert sent his womenfolk to Kildrummy Castle in Aberdeenshire while he

19

SCULPTURED HEAD WHICH WAS MODELLED
FROM A CAST OF ROBERT BRUCE'S SKULL

and some 200 followers took to the Breadalbane Hills of Perthshire. He had been outlawed by Edward I, excommunicated by Clement V and now, in September 1306, he was to be deprived of his family. Kildrummy Castle had been taken. His brother Neil was hung, drawn and beheaded; his sister Mary and Countess Isabella of Buchan were stuck in cages; and his wife and daughter were put in separate prisons. Robert was enough of a realist to admit that his present position in Scotland was quite hopeless. He did the expedient thing — he escaped from his homeland. Moving southwest, he reached Dunaverty Castle in Kintyre and from there sailed 14 miles to the island of Rathlin off the Irish coast. Robert's adventures as a fugitive during the winter of 1306-07 are described in Sir Walter Scott's "Lord of the Isles" and "Tales of a Grandfather."

Robert refused to concede defeat. In February 1307 he returned to his Earldom of Carrick to find it confiscated by the enemy. Regathering his supporters, Robert set about to raise an army to fight the English. Realizing his only chance of success against the English was to avoid pitched battle with an enemy that had the advantage of greater manpower and military equipment, Robert decided to concentrate all his energies on a sustained guerilla campaign against the relatively immobile army of occupation. Soon Robert was to prove himself a great national leader and military strategist in guerilla warfare.

In April 1307, Robert's forces ambushed John Mowbray's cavalry in Glen Trook, in Galloway, inflicting a defeat severe enough to re-establish his military credibility and open up the way to the north. On May 10th he gained a second victory. Though greatly outnumbered by the army of the experienced Aymer de Valence, Robert managed to outmaneuver him at Loudon Hill near Kilmarnoch. By confining de Valence's cavalry to an area unsuitable for maneuvering, Robert forced his enemy to flee to Bothwell, leaving his dead and wounded behind. Almost immediately this was followed by the defeat of the Earl of Gloucester, who in turn, fled to Ayr.

In his victories, Bruce was assisted by his principal lieutenant, Sir James Douglas, famous as the Black Douglas who became known as the terror of the English. He captured his own castle of Douglas from the English and utterly destroyed it. Gradually, more and more Scottish nobles joined Bruce: the Celtic Earls of Lennox and Atholl; Angus Og, the ancestor of Clan Donald, and the progenitors of the Campbells and Macleans. A series of Scottish victories followed, including a successful guerrilla action at Glentrool and another encounter at Loudon Hill, where Bruce showed conclusively that his spearmen could successfully oppose the English heavy cavalry.

Robert's victories inspired others to join the rebellion against the English and finally Edward I realized he had to start all over again subduing the Scots. Placing himself at the head of the powerful English army, Edward I resolved to crush for all time the Scottish resistance to his claim to overlordship. Conveniently for the Scots, Edward I (aged 68) died July 7, 1307 by the wayside (at Burgh-on-Sands) at the Solway Firth. With his dying breath he ordered that his bones were to be borne at the head of his army in a leather bag until Scotland had been crushed. But his son, Edward II made no effort to carry out his father's wishes. He promptly returned to London.

EDWARD II, 1307-1327

Edward II probably had adequate reasons for returning

22

to London after the death of his father, but he missed a great opportunity to accomplish what his father had set out to do — to totally subjugate the Scots. He further played into Robert's hand by replacing the formidable de Valence as Lieutenant of Scotland by John of Britanny. Robert was thus left relatively free, first to consolidate the ground his victories had gained, then to set about establishing himself in the pro-Balliol territories of Buchan, Argyll and Galloway.

On December 24, 1307, Robert, with 700 followers, defeated the Earl of Buchan, near Inverurie. Then he moved against Argyllshire. And he was expected. John MacDougall of Lorne, Lord of Argyll, determined to borrow Robert's fighting tactics prepared an ambush in the narrow Pass of Brander. By stationing his man on the slopes of Cruachan, they could fall on Robert's army as they arrived at the Pass. Instead, MacDougall was caught in his own trap simply because Robert was always several steps ahead of his adversaries. The Scottish king sent James Douglas with a Highland force further still up the slopes of Cruachan with the result that MacDougall's men were sandwiched on a hillside while the two parts of Robert's army closed in on them. Realizing their predicament, MacDougall's men fled across the river Awe, chased by Robert's army to Dunstaffnage, where they captured the castle.

With Buchan and Argyll in his control, Robert assigned his brother the task of subduing Galloway. This was accomplished with a bloody flourish. Now that Robert had a country to be king of, he held his first parliament — at St. Andrews on March 16-17, 1309. Here, the majority of the Scottish "communitas" endorsed him as the legitimate king of Scotland. However, the English still held castles of immense strategic importance, including Edinburgh and Stirling.

In 1309 a truce was effected by Pope Clement V and in February 1310, Robert was formally recognized as King of Scotland by the clergy of Scotland, in spite of his prior

STIRLING CASTLE

excommunication. With this backing, he set out to reduce the strongholds still held by the English. For the next four years, with the help of his brother Edward and the "Black" Douglas, Robert not only expelled English garrisons from Scottish castles but unleashed terror and destruction on the northern counties of England. Englishmen were forced to pay huge sums of money to buy peace from the revengeful Scots.

Linlithgow was taken from the English near the end of 1310; Dunbarton in October 1311; Perth on a bitter cold January night in 1313; Roxburgh and Edinburgh in 1314. Finally only Stirling Castle remained in English hands. Standing like a giant sentinel, guarding the most important gateway to the north, Stirling Castle was the key to Scotland's independence. Robert, recognizing this fact, had established a blockade of the castle in the summer of 1313. However, to the annoyance of King Robert, his brother, Edward Bruce, had made an agreement with Stirling's English governor, Sir Philip Mowbray, whereby the castle would be surrendered if the English had not relieved it by Midsummer Day.

Edward II, also recognized the importance of controlling Stirling Castle and assured the English governor that an English army would lift the siege. After all, if he could not muster the might of feudal England to relieve one castle by a specific date, then he would be revealed as a complete failure. And what better opportunity would he have to engage the Scots than in a pre-arranged pitched battle where his numerical superiority and heavy cavalry could not be matched by Robert's forces. Up to now, Robert's successes had been achieved precisely by avoiding pitched battles with the English.

Although the imprudent challenge accepted by Robert's brother, Edward, would place the Scots in a vulnerable position, Robert (the master of guerilla warfare) could not avoid a face-to-face conflict with the English. If he could not for once publicly demonstrate his strength in a pre-arranged pitched battle in his own kingdom then he would lose not only Stirling, but his hard-won reputation as an invincible battler. Both sides had everything to lose. Neither side intended to leave anything to chance.

King Edward II's relieving force consisted on nearly 20,000 men: 17,000 were archers (including the celebrated Welsh archers) and spear-wielding foot soldiers; 2,000 were English horsemen with chainmail and armor on quilted mounts; the balance were anti-Robert fanatics, including the Comyns and the MacDougalls. By contrast, Robert's army only consisted of about 6,000 foot soldiers armed with 14-foot pikes, axes, swords and bows. To face the English horsemen, he had some 500 light cavalry led by Sir Alexander Keith. However, Robert had military genius on his side and he planned the battle accordingly.

Robert chose the perfect site for blocking the expected English advance on Stirling Castle. He placed his men in a densely wooded area, with impassable scrub on his right and the stream-riddled and boggy Carse on his left. Behind him was Stirling castle and before him was the narrow Bannoch Burn which Edward II would have to cross. Bannoch Burn was not a formidable obstacle but Robert had made it so with ditches and cruelly-placed calthrops — four-pointed booby-traps that always landed spike-upwards to penetrate the feet of advancing cavalry. Bruce reckoned that Edward II would be forced to cross the Carse where his heavy cavalry and numerical strength would be of little advantage.

On Sunday Morning June 24, 1314, Robert addressed his troops. His words were preserved by his Chancellor Bernard de Linton (Abbot of Arbroath) who was present at Bannockburn. Bruce began: "My lords, my people, accustomed to enjoy that full freedom for which in times gone by the Kings of Scotland have fought many a battle! For eight years or more I have struggled with much labor for my right to the kingdom and for honourable liberty. I have lost brothers, friends and kinsmen. Your own kinsmen have been made captive, and bishops and priests are locked in prison. Our country's nobility has poured forth its blood in war."

CHAMPION OF SCOTLAND AGAINST ENGLISH AGGRESSION

Then, with his patriotic credentials established, Robert turned the attention of his men to the enemy: "Those barons you see before you, clad in mail, are bent upon destroying me and obliterating my kingdom, nay, our whole nation. They do not believe that we can survive. They glory in their warhorses and equipment ... For us, the name of the Lord must be our hope of victory in battle. This day is a day of rejoicing ... With our Lord Jesus Christ as commander, Saint Andrew and the martyr Saint Thomas shall fight today with the saints of Scotland for the honour of their country and their nation."

As the Scots faced the English in the dawn of Midsummer Day they knelt to receive the blessing of the Abbot of Inchaffray. The English king, watching from a distance, is reported to have said: "See they are asking for mercy." The answer an aide gave was: "True, but not from you. Those men will win or perish." Before the day had ended, the Scots had won their only major battle in the centuries of strife between England and Scotland. The English, trapped in the impossible narrow confines of the Bannoch Burn and the peatbogs of the Carse, were forced to

REPRESENTATION OF THE BATTLE OF BANNOCKBURN
FROM A 15TH CENTURY M.S
(On the ground may be the Englishman, de Bohun, being killed by Bruce himself)

retreat. Then, at the critical moment, Robert's cavalry and a reserve division of Scots surged forward so explosively that the rapidly retreating English became unavoidable targets for their own back-line archers.

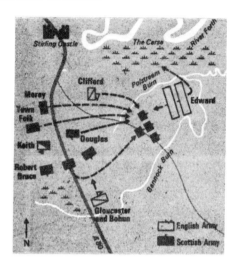

Finally, Edward II decided he had had enough and rushed for the safety of his garrison in Stirling Castle. But Sir Philip would not let him in so the English king had to flee towards Dunbar. The English troops that tried to follow their king were forced suicidally into the waters of the Forth: the English left fell back, like human debris, into the Bannock Burn. Edward II's able general, the Earl of Gloucester, was killed and many valuable hostages captured by the Scots. Among these was the Earl of Hereford, whom Robert exchanged for his wife, daughter, and friend, the Bishop of Glasgow. Over 200,000 pieces of equipment were abandoned and left to the Scots.

Robert now turned the tables on the English, invading and devastating their country as they had devastated his. He also carried the war over to Ireland. The Irish, encouraged by the English successes in Scotland, had bestowed the Crown of Ireland on the English king's brother, Edward. However, when in 1322 Edward II attempted another

EQUESTRIAN STATUE OF ROBERT BRUCE
ERECTED AT BANNOCKBURN IN 1964 ON
THE ANNIVERSARY OF HIS GREATEST VICTORY

invasion of Scotland, he was chased back into Yorkshire, losing his personal baggage in the process.

Although it was to be fourteen years before the war was officially over, there was no doubt that Robert was unquestionably in control of his kingdom. He had shown he could defeat the English by guerilla tactics or in pitched battle if need be. He had his wife back (she was to produce a male heir, David, in 1324) and an unshakeable grasp on his throne. On April 25, 1315, at the Parliament of Ayr, the succession to the Scottish throne was unanimously settled on Robert Bruce and his heirs.

The shameless desertion of King Edward II from the field of battle caused the name of "Bannockburn" to be a source of embarrassment to the English for a long time after. But, in spite of his defeat, Edward II was not going to give up his efforts to subjugate the Scots. He had still another card to play — a clever one. Pope John XXII was the newly-installed Pope and held his purple court just across the Channel at Avignon. The Pope was soon gratified by the arrival of the English ambassadors, whose master seemed most anxious to make up for a previous neglect. At least, that is what it looked like when they began to lavish a king's ransom of precious stones and jewels on the Pope.

It was not long before the "Vicar of Christ" had entered into the spirit of things. In 1317 A.D. Edward II reaped his reward. A couple of cardinals arrived from Avignon armed with a pontifical order to establish a truce between the two countries — the first step towards ousting Robert Bruce as king. Not daring themselves to put foot upon Scottish soil, their illustrious lordships persuaded a local friar to deliver the papal command to Robert. The poor man reached Robert only to be informed that as the letters were not addressed to the "King" they could not be received.

Realizing the delicacy of his position, the unfortunate monk requested a safe conduct for his return journey. Instead he received this advice: "Terram evacuare quancitius poterat" —or "clear out as quickly as you can." The story is told that on his way back he was waylayed by some of Robert's men. They stripped him and, to the astonishment of the citizens, he was seen to wander naked into the streets of Berwick. When word reached the Pope he was furious and instructed his cardinals to excommunicate the impudent monarch for "sacrilege."

Robert continued his struggle against the English by capturing the fortified city of Berwick and besieging the Castle which surrendered three months later. Then followed the capture of three Northumberland Castles: Wark, Harbottle and Mitford. In an endeavor to counteract the Scot's victories, Edward II mounted several skirmishes against the Scots that proved ineffective. With 8,000 men he failed to recapture Berwick Castle and was finally persuaded to remove himself from the Border.

In October 1318, Robert heard that his brother, Edward had been killed and his army defeated at the battle of Dunkald. This raised the question of succession again. In December 1318, at a parliament held in Scone, the succession was settled on Robert Steward. He had been born in March 1316, as his mother, Marjory, died after falling from a horse. As the result of his continued failure to crush the Scottish resistance, King Edward II reluctantly agreed to a two-year truce, on December 25, 1319. However, he continued to emphasize Robert's iniquity to the Pope. And when four Scottish bishops ignored a papal summons, they were therefore excommunicated along with their king.

The Scottish king's position was now so strong that foreign countries began to recognize him and his country's independence. However, Robert recognized that if peace was ever to be restored between England and Scotland, the Pope would have to be made to see the wisdom of a negotiated settlement and to use his influence upon King Edward II. The Scots, having fought so hard for their independence, were ready to make a declaration of their cause to anyone, even an unsympathetic Pope.

In April of the year 1320 A.D., King Robert Bruce called the Scottish Parliament into session, at Arbroath Abbey, to hammer out a letter of protest to the Pope. The letter, composed in memorable Latin prose, recorded the great antiquity of the Scottish people and how they had always been ruled by their own kings. Beside, they objected, the King of England was once divided among seven or more kings. Also, they reminded the Pope of the shameful English contention that they had found it impossible to free the Holy Land from the heathen on account of the war they were having with their neighbors. The true reason, the Scots suggested, was that in the subjugation of their smaller neighbors, the English reckoned the advantage nearer and the resistance feeble.

The letter described Robert Bruce as a king, "who, that he might free his people and heritage from the hands of the enemy, rose like another Joshua or Maccabeus, and cheerfully endured toil and weariness, hunger and peril." And to emphasize that Robert Bruce was king by common consent and no tyrant, the letter assured the Pope that "were he to abandon the task to which he has set his hand or to show any disposition to subject us or our realm to the King of England or the English, we would instantly strive to expel him as our enemy and ... choose another king to rule over us."

THE ARBROATH DECLARATION

The celebrated letter, known as the "Declaration of Arbroath" and dated April 6, 1320, was sent to Pope John XXII in Avignon. The Pope acknowledged receipt of the letter and was apparently somewhat mollified by the declaration, because he promptly suspended his proceedings against the Scots. He even went so far as to induce the English king to drop his case against Robert. However, King Edward II refused to conclude a peace settlement with the Scots and in August 1322, when the two-year-old truce was over, again invaded Scotland.

Edward II did manage to reach Edinburgh where he sacked Holyrood Abbey. Anticipating this invasion, Robert had cleared Lothian of cattle and grain so that, lacking food, the English would have to return to England. When Edward's retreating army attempted to do to Melrose Abbey what they had done to Holyrood, they were attacked and scattered by the waiting Douglas clan. Robert personally led

34

a large army that followed the English over the border and nearly captured Edward at Rievaulx Abbey. Despite his manifest and repeated failures, Edward II still stubbornly refused to sign a peace treaty.

On January 20, 1327 Edward II was deposed and murdered. This is believed to have been instigated by his wife Isabel and her lover, Mortimer. He was succeeded by his 14-year-old son, Edward III, whose coronation was held in February. The Scots celebrated the event by attacking Norham Castle. Further English attempts at invasion of Scotland came to nothing, only provoking vigorous counter-attacks. The English were now growing tired of the war. Continuing victories against the English forced the regents for Edward III to seek peace. Although earlier efforts at mediation had failed, another English envoy was sent to Norham to sue for peace.

Robert, in return for peace, asked for recognition for himself and his heirs as Kings of Scotland, a marriage between his baby son, David, and Edward III's little sister, Joanna; a military alliance and help in lifting the excommunication the Pope had imposed upon him. In return, he offered £20,000 as the price of peace. Robert's offer was magnanimous enough to be acceptable to the English.

On March 17, 1328 the Treaty of Edinburgh was concluded at Holyrood Abbey where Robert lay ill. It was ratified at Northampton on May 4th. The treaty allowed that; "Scotland according to its ancient bounds in the days of Alexander III should remain to Robert, King of the Scots, and his heirs free and divided from England, without any subjection, servitude, claim or demand whatsoever." Edward III's sister Joanna was married to David, Robert's young son, on July 12, 1328.

On June 7, 1329, the 55 year old King of the Scots died at his home in Cardross Village on the west side of the river Leven. At the time of his death in Cardross, Pope John XXII was preparing a bull that gave complete papal recognition to Robert I and his successors as kings of an independent Scotland. The theory that Robert died of leprosy is difficult to reconcile with the fact that Robert's friends had access to his presence until the last.

CAST OF THE SKULL OF ROBERT BRUCE

Robert's body was buried in Dunfermline Abbey to lie beside his gracious ancestress St. Margaret, but only after his heart had been removevd and given to his great friend, Sir James Douglas. From his deathbed, Robert revealed he had once vowed to go on a crusade to the Holy Land, but "seeing, therefore, that my body cannot go to achieve what my heart desires, I will send my heart instead of my body, to accomplish my vow." Douglas took the heart instead of his body, to accomplish the vow. Douglas took the heart in a silver casket with him on his crusade to fight against the enemies of Christendom. Douglas was killed and the heart lost. Yet, both were eventually recovered and brought back to Scotland. Douglas lies in St. Bride's Kirk in Douglasdale, and the heart of the great Patriot King of Scotland in Melrose Abbey, the exact whereabouts unknown.

AERIAL VIEW OF MELROSE ABBEY FROM THE SOUTH-EAST

Wallace, a country gentleman, started the fight for Scotland's freedom and Robert Bruce finished it. In doing so, Robert gave Scotland the most outstanding document in its national history — the "Declaration of Arbroath." This great declaration, described by Sir Walter Scott as "worthy of being written in letters of gold," carries a message of supreme importance for the world today. It is enshrined, yellow with age, in Scotland's Record Office in Edinburgh. In it occurs the ringing phrase: "We fight not for glory nor for honours; but only and alone we fight for freedom, which no good man surrenders but with his life."

One Scottish historian dramatically relates the signing of the document: "In their colorful robes, the Abbot of Arbroath, Bernard de Linton, followed by the Bishops of St.

MELROSE ABBEY — AS IT MIGHT HAVE LOOKED IN THE 15TH CENTURY FROM A DRAWING BY ALAN SORRELL (1957)

Andres, Aberdeen, and Dunkeld, paced up the nave. King Robert took his place on a dais. One by one, his barons came forward and affixed their seals to the great charter which was to make its long journey to France and light a torch in Europe that has never been extinguished. After the last seal had been affixed to the parchment, Robert and the Abbot read it together: "For so long as a hundred of us are left alive, we will yield in no least way."

ILLUSTRATION OF THE DRAFTING OF THE DECLARATION OF ARBROATH
TAKEN FROM A STAMP PRODUCED BY THE G.P.O.

THE SCOTTISH DECLARATION OF INDEPENDENCE

Written in fluent Latin, the Declaration of Arbroath reads in English as follows:

━━━━━━━━━━━━━━━

To the Most Holy Father in Christ and Lord, the Lord John, by divine providence Supreme Pontift of the Holy Roman and Universal Church, his humble and devout sons Duncan, Earl of Fife, Thomas Randolph, Earl of Moray, Lord of Man and of Annandale, Patrick Dunbar, Earl of March, Malise, Earl of Strathearn, Macolm, Earl of Lennos, William, earl of Ross, Magnus, Earl of Caithness and Orkney, and William, Earl of Sutherland; Walter, Stewart of Scotland, William Soules, Butler of Scotland, James, Lord of Douglas, Roger Mowbray, David, Lord of Brechin, David Graham, Ingram Umfraville, John Menteith, guardian of the earldom of Menteith, Alexander Fraser, Gilbert Hay, Constable of Scotland, Robert Keith, Marischal of Scotland, Henry St. Clair, John Graham, David Lindsay, William Oliphant, Patrick Graham, John Fenton, William Abernathy, David Wemyss, William Mushet, Fergus of Ardrossan,

Eustace Maxwell, William Ramsay, William Mowat, Alan Murray, Donald Campbell, John Cameron, Reginald Cheyne, Alexander Seton, Andrew Leslie, and Alexander Straiton, and the other barons and freeholders and the whole community of the realm of Scotland send all manner of filial reverence, with devout kisses of his blessed feet.

Most Holy Father and Lord, we know and from the chronicles and books of the ancients we find that among other famous nations our own, the Scots, has been graced with widespread renown. They journeyed from Greater Scythia by way of the Tyrrhenian Sea and the Pillars of Hercules, and dwelt for a long course of time in Spain among the most savage tribes, but nowhere could they be subdued by any race, however barbarous. Thence they came, twelve hunred years after the people of Israel crossed the Red Sea, to their home in the west where they still live today. The Britons they first drove out, the Picts they utterly destroyed, and even though very often assailed by the Norwegians, the Danes and the English, they took possession of that home with many victories and untold efforts; and, as the historians of old time bear witness, they have held it free of all bondage ever since. In their kingdom there have reigned one hundred and thirteen kings of their own royal stock, the line unbroken by a single foreigner.

The high qualities and deserts of these people, were they not otherwise manifest, gain glory enough from this: that the King of kings and Lord of lords, our Lord Jesus Christ, after His Passion and Resurrection, called them, even though settled in the uttermost parts of the earth, almost the first to His most holy faith. Nor would He have them confirmed in that faith by merely anyone but by the first of His Apostles by calling—though second or third in rank—the most gentle Saint Andrew, the Blessed Peter's brother, and desired him to keep them under his protection as their patron for ever.

The Most Holy Fathers your predecessors gave careful heed to these things and bestowed many favours and numerous privileges on this same kingdom and people, as being the special charge of the Blessed Peter's brother. Thus our nation under their protection did indeed live in freedom and peace up to the time when that mighty prince the King of the English, Edward, the father of the one who reigns today, when our kingdom had no head and our people harboured no malice or treachery and were then unused to wars or invasions, came in the guise of a friend and ally to harass them as an enemy. The deeds of cruelty, massacre, violence, pillage, arson, imprisoning prelates, burning down monasteries, robbing and killing monks and nuns, and yet other outrages without number which

41

he committed against our people, sparing neither age nor sex, religion nor rank, no one could describe nor fully imagine unless he had seen them with his own eyes.

But from these countless evils we have been set free, by the help of Him who though He afflicts yet heals and restores, by our most tireless Prince, King and Lord, the Lord Robert. He, that his people and his heritage might be delivered out of the hands of our enemies, met toil and fatigue, hunger and peril, like another Maccabaeus or Joshua, and bore them cheerfully. Him, too, divine providence, his right of succession according to our laws and customs which we shall maintain to the death, and the due consent and assent of us all have made our Prince and King. To him, as to the man by whom salvation has been wrought unto our people, we are bound both by law and by his merits that our freedom may be still maintained, and by him, come what may, we mean to stand.

Yet if he should give up what he has begun, and agree to make us or our kingdom subject to the King of England or the English, we should exert ourselves at once to drive him out as our enemy and a subverter of his own rights and ours, and make some other man who was well able to defend us our King; for, as long as but a hundred of us remain alive, never will we on any conditions be brought under English rule. It is in truth not for glory, nor riches, nor honours that we are fighting, but for freedom—for that alone, which no honest man gives up but with life itself.

Therefore it is, Reverend Father and Lord, that we beseech your Holiness with our most earnest prayers and suppliant hearts, inasmuch as you will in your sincerity and goodness consider all this, that, since with Him Whose vice-gerent on earth you are there is neither weighing nor distinction of Jew and Greek, Scotsman or Englishman, you will look with the eyes of a father on the troubles and privations brought by the English upon us and upon the Church of God. May it please you to admonish and exhort the King of the English, who ought be satisfied with what belongs to him since England used once to be enough for seven kings or more, to leave us Scots in peace, who live in this poor little Scotland, beyond which there is no dwelling-place at all, and covet nothing but our own. We are sincerely willing to do anything for him, having regard to our condition, that we can, to win peace for ourselves.

This truly concerns you, Holy Father, since you see the savagery of the heathen raging against the Christians, as the sins of Christians have indeed deserved, and the frontiers of Christendom being pressed inward every day; and how much it will tarnish your holiness's memory if (which God forbid) the Church suffers eclipse or scandal in any branch of it during your time, you must perceive. Then rouse the Christian princes who for false reasons pretend that they cannot go to the help of the Holy Land because of wars they have on hand with their neighbours. The real reason that prevents them is that in making war on their smaller neighbours they find quicker profit and weaker resistance. But how cheerfully our Lord the King and we too would go there if the King of the English would leave us in peace, He from Whom nothing is hidden well knows; and we profess and declare it to you as the Vicar of Christ and to all Christendom.

But if your Holiness puts too much faith in the tales the English tell and will not give sincere belief to all this, nor refrain from favouring them to our prejudice, then the slaughter of bodies, the perdition of souls, and all the other misfortunes that will follow, inflicted by them on us and by us on them, will, we believe, be surely laid by the most High to your charge.

To conclude, we are and shall ever be, as far as duty calls us, ready to do your will in all things, as obedient sons to you as His Vicar; and to Him as the Supreme King and Judge, we commit the maintenance of our cause, casting our cares upon Him and firmly trusting that He will inspire us with courage and bring our enemies to nought.

May the Most High preserve you to His Holy Church in holiness and health and grant you length of days.

Given at the monastery of Arbroath in Scotland on the sixth day of the month of April in the year of grace thirteen hundred and twenty and the fifteenth year of the reign of our King aforesaid.

King James VI of Scotland (King James I of England) claimed that the Lord had made him ''King over Israel'' and upon the gold coin of his day, (the Jacobus) he had inscribed in Latin the prophecy of Ezekiel 37:22 ''I will make of them one nation.''

AN ANALYSIS

From the Declaration of Arbroath we discover that Robert Bruce and his knights whose seals are affixed to that famous document, date their beginnings as a nation one thousand two hundred years after the outgoing (Exodus — 1453 B.C.) of the "people of Israel." Thus, they claim descent from the Israelites in Egypt. The validity of such a claim is supported by many historians who point to Israelite presence (particularly of Dan and Judah) in the British Isles at a very early date, even before the Exodus.

All the Israelites in Egypt did not accompany Moses into the Promised Land. Hecataeus of Abdera (sixth century B.C. historian — quoted by the Greek historian Diodorus Siculus — 50 B.C. — 1,27,46,55) says: "the most distinguished of the expelled foreigners (from Egypt followed Danaus and Cadmus into Greece; but the greater number were led by Moses into Judea." According to Petavius, (History of the World) Danaus was the son of Bela, (Belus) a sojourner in Egypt. His brother was Egyptus. Danaus was informed by an oracle that his brother would slay him; he fled, taking with him his daughters (colonists) and came to Greece three years after the death of Joseph. This was about 148 years before the Exodus.

The "History of Ireland" by Moore, states that the ancient Irish, called the "Danai" or "Danes," separated from Israel around the time of the Exodus from Egypt, crossed to Greece and then invaded Ireland. Historians call these people the "Tuatha De Danaan" (Tribe of Dan). The "Leabha Gabhala" or "Book of Conquests of Ireland," give their earlier name as "Tuatha De," meaning "People of God."

On Ptolemy's ancient map of Ireland we find, in the north-eastern corner of the island, such names as "Dan-Sowar" (Dan's Resting Place) and "Dan Sobairse" (Dan's Habitation). Gladstone's "Juventus Mundi" and the "old

44

Psalter of Cashel" both state that some of the Grecian Danai left Greece and invaded Ireland. Petanius (sixth century B.C.) speaks of the Danaï as being Hebrew people, originally from Egypt, who colonized Ireland.

The Milesians, who invaded Ireland circa 1000 B.C. and subjugated the Tuatha De Danaan (People of God), were also a branch of the Hebrew stem. It was from a later group of Milesians (about the 5th century B.C.) that Ireland received one of its earliest names — "Scota." The Milesians in general were commonly called "Scotti" or "Scots" by the early Latin Historians and poets. It was said that the name "Scots" came from "Scota," a daughter of a far eastern king (Zedekiah) who married Gathelus, a Milesian prince. It was from this union that the kings of Tara (Ireland) were descended. The marriage is said to have occured during the reign of a Pharaoh who was "drowned" in the Red Sea. This would have been the Pharaoh Hophra (XXI Dynasty) who provided refuge for Jeremiah and the daughters of King Zedekiah of Judah. The Pharaoh was later murdered in his boat in 566 B.C.

The Chronicles of Scotland record the story of their ancestor Gathelus leaing Egypt with his wife (Scota) and friends this way. Rather than "to abyde ye manifest wengenace of goddis" (reference to God's judgement on the remnant that had fled to Egypt to escape Nebuchadnezzar) and travelling by sea (Mediterranean), after, "lang tyme he landit in ane part of Spayne callit Lusitan." (later called Partungall). After this he built the city of Brigance (in Spain) and "callit his subdittis (subjects) Scottis in honour and afeccioun of his wyiff."

Many historians, today, erroneously refer to the Milesians as "Celts" and Gaels." Actually, they were only the forerunners of the Celtic tribes that wound their way across Europe from the east, turbulently meeting and finally blending in amity, and flowing onward in one great Gaelic stream into the island of Britain. The Celts were kinsmen but mainly of the later westward migrations of the Israelites as they left the regions of Gozan (Assyrian captivity) by way of the upper Euphrates gorge. (II Esdras 13:43) Most of them crossed the Black Sea to the Carpathean Mountains, called "Arsareth" in the Apocrypha. From there, they migrated up the Danube into Central Europe and became known as "Celts" and Gauls."

(Note: Archaeological evidence in the form of clay cuneiform tablets of the "Royal Correspondence of the Assyrian Empire" (Missing Links Discovered in Assyrian Tablets — 1985 Capt) have established the fact that the Celts are the Cimmerians-Israelites called, during their captivity by the Assyrians, "Gimira" or "Gamera.")

Between 400-100 B.C., the Celts poured into Britain to form the "bed-rock" of the British race. One group, in Spain, known as "Iberes" (the Gaelic name for Hebrews) moved into Ireland, naming the island "Hibernia" a name that still exists. From them came the High Kings of Tara that ruled Ireland for several centuries.

About 500 A.D., the Scottish King Fergus Mor Mc Erc (the Great) of the Gaelic Kingdom of Dalriada (in Ireland) left his Irish palace at Dunseverick and invaded the south-western part of the Pictish Kingdom in northern Britain. The Picts (in Gaelic, "Cruithne," meaning "Pictured Men," because they painted themselves) were a confederation of Celtic tribes. They spoke a slightly different language than Celtic and had different customs from the Gaels of the west and the Britains of Strathclyde, in the south.

The Scots (from Ireland) were successful in driving the Picts north, out of Argyllshire. They set up their new capital inside the ramparts of an old Pictish fort on the hill of Dunadd. From there, Fergus ruled both halves of his kingdom, one in Ireland and the other in Scotland. For a time, the Scottish kingdom of Dalriada appears to have been dependent upon Irish Dalriada. But, about 575 A.D. Aidan (son of King Gabran) secured its independence and was

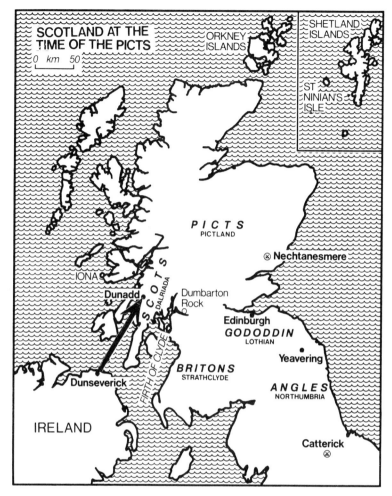

SCOTLAND AT THE TIME OF THE PICTS

0 km 50

SHETLAND ISLANDS

ORKNEY ISLANDS

ST NINIAN'S ISLE

PICTS
PICTLAND

⊗ Nechtanesmere

IONA

DALRIADA

Dunadd

Dumbarton Rock

Edinburgh

GODODDIN
LOTHIAN

Yeavering

BRITONS
STRATHCLYDE

ANGLES
NORTHUMBRIA

Dunseverick

FIRTH OF CLYDE

IRELAND

Catterick
⊗

crowned King of Scotland upon the "Stone Lia Fail." (Stone of Destiny). One of Aidan's successor, Kenneth, became king of the Picts about 843 A.D., and gradually the name "Dalraida," both in Ireland and Scotland fell into disuse.

Many of the Scottish and Irish legends, as well as the Declaration of Arbroath, claim that the remote ancestors of the Scots came from Scythia. This was the ancient name for south Russia. This had led some authorities to believe that they were derived from the Scythian branch of the "Gamera" (Israelites). However, this is not the case. What is now Scythia was once inhabited by Cimmerians and there

47

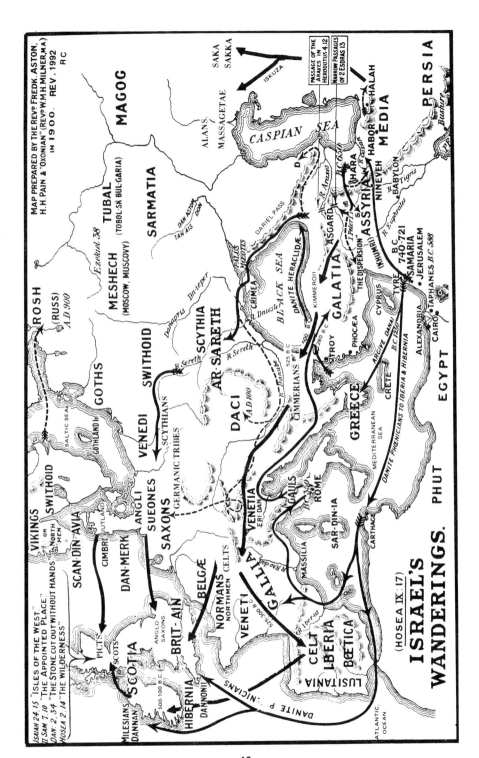

ISRAEL'S WANDERINGS.

(HOSEA IX:17)

are still traces of the Cimmerians in Scythia: one finds, for instance, remains of a fortification, a Cimmerian strait, the Cimmerian Peninsula, and a tract of land called Cimmeria.

Language also indicates the Cimmerians (Celts) did not originate from the Scythians. The Anglo-Saxon descendants of the Scythians have a totally difference language from the Gaelic and Welsh languages of the Celts. Although both languages can be traced to the Hebrew, their complete separation for centuries and their totally different contacts account for the differences.

To summarize — we find from historical records and archaeological evidence, that there were several migrations of Hebrew peoples arriving in Ireland at different times and under different names. They came as the Tuatha De Danaan — Milesians and Celts — and apparently, amalgamated. Yet, in fact, they were the same peoples ethnically. The migrations of these early people from Ireland to northern Britain (around the 6th century A.D.) established the Celtic kingdom of the Scots where five centuries later, their descendants founded the nation and kingdom of Scotland.

In tracing the origin of the Scots to the ancient Hebrew people we see the fulfillment of many Bible prophecies:

As for me, behold, my covenant is with thee, and thou shalt be a father of many nations ... and I will make nations of thee, and kings shall come out of thee." (Gen. 17:4,6)

"Moreover, I will appoint a place for my people Israel, and will plant them, that they may dwell in a place of their own, and move no more; neither shall the children of wickedness afflict them any more, as beforetime." (II Sam, 7:10)

"For the Lord shall smite Israel as a reed is shaken in the water, and he shall root up Israel out of this good land, which he gave to their fathers, and shall scatter them beyond the River (Euphrates), *because they have made their groves* (idolatrous symbols) *provoking the Lord to anger."* (I Kings 14:15)

For, lo, I will command, and I will sift the house of Israel among all nations, like as corn is sifted in a sieve, yet shall not the least grain fall upon the earth." (Amos 9:9)

"For thy seed shall be as the dust of the earth, and thou shalt spread abroad to the west, and to the east, and to the north, and to the south: and in thee and in they seed shall all the families of the earth be blessed." (Gen. 28:14)

Bring forth the royal diadem,
And crown Him Lord of all.
Ye chosen seed of Israel's race,
Ye ransomed from the fall,
Hail Him who saves you by His grace,
And crown Him Lord of all.

SCOTLAND

From Pict and Scot and Celt and Briton,
And Angle, Viking, Norman diversity
We Scots in time from these were forged
Now conscious of our common unity.

Skirl of pipe and swirl of kilt –
A joy to us, a joy to others –
Fond memory of our mountain hame [home]
Unites all Scots as band of brothers.

See Bruce and Wallace nobly fight
To free our folk and lochs and bens
While Burns and Scott and Raeburn too
Make known our land of lovely glens.

SCOTTISH ROYAL ARMS

The Banner or Arms of Scotland consists of a golden flag with one red rampant (an animal standing erect on the hind legs) Lion displayed within a double tressure (the diminitive of the orle-being half its size). It is supported by Unicorns with golden cornets (the badge or cognizance of Princes and Peers) on their necks, with golden chains attached. The chains remain loose-significant of a people freed from their bondage (Israel was referred to as a Unicorn — Num. 14:19; 23:22, 24:8,9; Deut. 33:17). The Unicorns each support flag staffs, one bearing the banner of Scotland and the other the flag of St. Andrew. "In Defence," the motto at the top, and within the scroll we can see the little Lion (crowned) of Judah, holding in his paws the sword and sceptre — representing the Lord Jesus Christ. The scroll beneath reads; "Nemo Me Imune Lacessit," meaning, "No One Attacks Me With Impunity."

51

ROBERT THE BRUCE   WILLIAM WALLACE

(1274-1329)   (1270-1305)

MEMORIALS AT MAIN ENTRANCE TO EDINBURGH CASTLE

Bonnie Scotland

In verse

Scotland Yet

The heath waves wild upon her hills,
  And, foaming frae the fells,
Her fountains sing o' freedom still,
  As they dance down the dells;
And weel I loo the land, my lads,
  That's girded by the sea;—
Then Scotland's vales and Scotland's dales
  And Scotland's hills for me;—
We'll drink a cup to Scotland yet,
  Wi' a' the honours three.

HENRY SCOTT RIDDEL 1798–1870

Songs of Travel

In the highlands, in the country places,
Where the old plain men have rosy faces,
And the young fair maidens
Quiet eyes;
Where essential silence cheers and blesses,
And for ever in the hill-recesses
Her more lovely music
Broods and dies.

ROBERT BURNS
Original model for the colosal bronze statue at Irvine

My Heart's in the Highlands

My heart's in the Highlands, my heart is not here;
My heart's in the Highlands a-chasing the deer;
Chasing the wild deer, and following the roe,
My heart's in the Highlands, wherever I go.
Farewell to the Highlands, farewell to the North,
The birth-place of valour, the country of worth;
Wherever I wander, wherever I rove,
The hills of the Highlands for ever I love.

ROBERT BURNS 1759–1796

Bonnie Bell

The smiling spring comes in rejoicing,
And surly winter grimly flies:
Now crystal clear are the falling waters,
And bonnie blue are the sunny skies;
Fresh o'er the mountains breaks forth the morning,
The ev'ning gilds the ocean's swell;
All creatures joy in the sun's returning,
And I rejoice in my bonnie Bell.

ROBERT BURNS 1759–1796

SIR WALTER SCOTT WITH HIS FRIENDS

Auld Lang Syne

Should auld acquaintance be forget,
　And never brought to min'?
Should auld acquaintance be forgot,
　And auld lang syne?

　　For auld lang syne, my dear.
　　For auld lang syne,
　　We'll tak a cup o' kindness yet,
　　For auld lang syne.

We twa hae run about the braes,
　And pu'd the gowans fine;
But we've wander'd mony a weary foot
　Sin' auld lang syne.

We twa hae paidled i' the burn,
　From morning sun till dine;
But seas between us braid hae roar'd
　Sin' auld lang syne.

And there's a hand, my trusty fiere,
　And gie's a hand o' thine;
And we'll tak a right guid-willie waught,
　For auld lang syne.

And surely ye'll be your pint-stowp,
　And surely I'll be mine;
And we'll tak a cup o' kindness yet
　For auld lang syne.

ROBERT BURNS 1759–1796

57

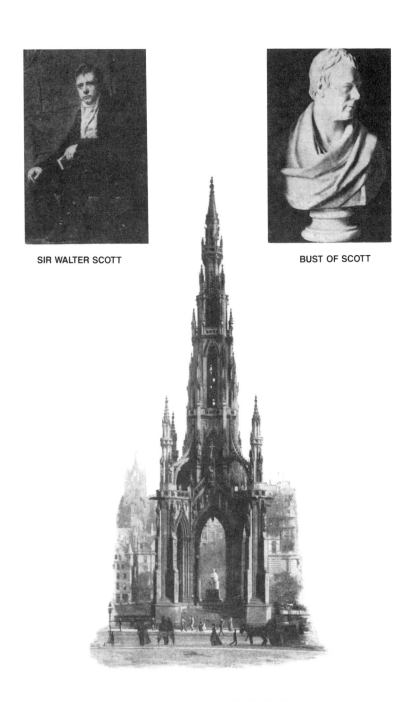

SIR WALTER SCOTT

BUST OF SCOTT

SCOTT'S MONUMENT AT EDINBURGH

Breathes there the man, with soul so dead,
Who never to himself hath said,
    This is my own, my native land!
Whose heart hath ne'er within him burn'd,
As home his footsteps he hath turn'd,
    From wandering on a foreign strand!
If such there breathe, go, mark him well;
For him no Minstrel raptures swell;
High though his titles, proud his name,
Boundless his wealth as wish can claim;
Despite those titles, power, and pelf,
The wretch, concentred all in self,
Living, shall forfeit fair renown,
And, doubly dying, shall go down
To the vile dust, from whence he sprung,
Unwept, unhonour'd, and unsung.

O Caledonia! stern and wild,
Meet nurse for a poetic child!
Land of brown heath and shaggy wood,
Land of the mountain and the flood,
Land of my sires! what mortal hand
Can e'er untie the filial band,
That knits me to thy rugged strand!
Still as I view each well-known scene,
Think what is now, and what hath been,
Seems as, to me, of all bereft,
Sole friends thy woods and streams were left;
And thus I love them better still,
Even in extremity of ill.

SIR WALTER SCOTT 1771–1832

The Wooer's Visit

My native Scotland! Oh, thy northern hills,
    Thy dark brown hills, are fondly dear to me;
And aye a warmth my swelling bosom fills
    For all the filial souls that cling to thee!
    Pure be their loves as human love can be;
And still be worthy of their native land
    The little beings nursed beside their knee,—
What may at length their country's guardians stand,
And own the undaunted heart, and lift the unconquer'd
        hand!

WILLIAM KNOX 1789–1825

It's Hame, and it's Hame

It's hame, and it's hame, hame fain wad I be,
An' it's hame, hame, hame, to my ain countree!
When the flower is i' the bud and the leaf is on the tree,
The lark shall sing me hame in my ain countree;
It's hame, and it's hame, hame fain wad I be,
An' it's hame, hame, hame, to my ain countree!

ALLAN CUNNINGHAM 1784–1842

The Cotter's Saturday Night

From scenes like these old Scotia's grandeur springs,
  That makes her loved at home, revered abroad;
Princes and lords are but the breath of kings,
  'An honest man's the noblest work of God':
And certes, in fair virtue's heavenly road,
  The cottage leaves the palace far behind;
What is a lordling's pomp?—a cumbrous load,
  Disguising oft the wretch of human kind,
Studied in arts of hell, in wickedness refined!

ROBERT BURNS 1759–1796

The bonnie banks o' Loch Lomon'.

By yon bonnie banks and yon bonnie braes,
  Where the sun shines bright on Loch Lomon';
Oh, we twa hae pass'd sae mony blithesome days,
  On the bonnie, bonnie banks o' Loch Lomon'.

(Chorus): Oh! ye'll tak' the high road and I'll tak' the
      low road,
    An' I'll be in Scotland before ye;
    But wae is my heart until we meet again,
      On the bonnie, bonnie banks o' Loch Lomon'.

TRADITIONAL JACOBITE AIR

TO SCOTLAND

The breath of thee, Scotland, is fragrant;
  The scent of thy hair
All myrtle and heather, with vagrant
  Wild sweets on the air;
And rowans thy cheeks, and red roses
  Thy lips are, and bluebells thine eyes:
Thy beauty the secret encloses
  Of moorland and skies.
Of the calm and the storm of the ocean
  That girdles thy shore
Thy moods have the stillness and motion,
  The silence and roar.
Thy spring hath the whiteness of blossom,
  Of snowdrop and foam,
And snowy in winter thy bosom,
  Thou warriors' home.

O Queen of the North! In thy story
  What heroes there dwell!
There is tragedy, mystery, glory;
  There is Heaven and Hell;
There are visions of seers, and the thunder
  Of battle, and harpers and bards,
And pibrochs of infinite wonder,
  And honour, and valour that guards.
There is truth, there is fortitude, fealty,
  The martyrdom loyal hearts bear;
There is love that surpasseth in lealty: —
  There was Bruce, there was Deirdre the Fair;
There was Charles in the dim corries ranging,
  There was Flora to cherish and save:
Though the world change, thy Soul is not changing,
  Thou faithful and brave!

GENEALOGY OF THE SCOTTISH KINGS

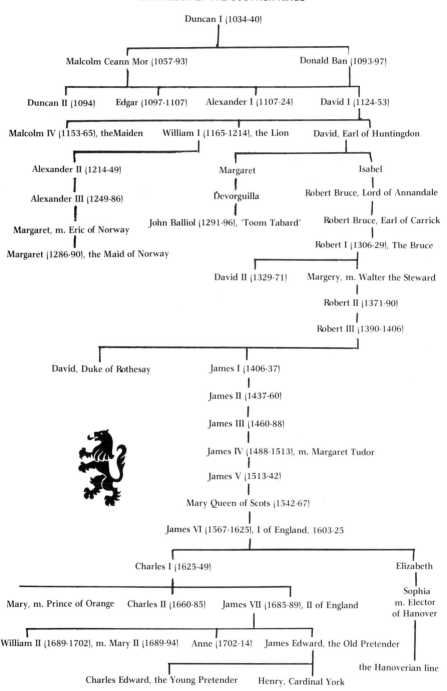

Duncan I (1034-40)

Malcolm Ceann Mor (1057-93)   Donald Ban (1093-97)

Duncan II (1094)   Edgar (1097-1107)   Alexander I (1107-24)   David I (1124-53)

Malcolm IV (1153-65), theMaiden   William I (1165-1214), the Lion   David, Earl of Huntingdon

Alexander II (1214-49)   Margaret   Isabel

Alexander III (1249-86)   Devorguilla   Robert Bruce, Lord of Annandale

Margaret, m. Eric of Norway   John Balliol (1291-96), 'Toom Tabard'   Robert Bruce, Earl of Carrick

Margaret (1286-90), the Maid of Norway   Robert I (1306-29), The Bruce

David II (1329-71)   Margery, m. Walter the Steward

Robert II (1371-90)

Robert III (1390-1406)

David, Duke of Rothesay   James I (1406-37)

James II (1437-60)

James III (1460-88)

James IV (1488-1513), m. Margaret Tudor

James V (1513-42)

Mary Queen of Scots (1542-67)

James VI (1567-1625), I of England, 1603-25

Charles I (1625-49)   Elizabeth

Sophia
m. Elector
of Hanover

Mary, m. Prince of Orange   Charles II (1660-85)   James VII (1685-89), II of England

William II (1689-1702), m. Mary II (1689-94)   Anne (1702-14)   James Edward, the Old Pretender

the Hanoverian line

Charles Edward, the Young Pretender   Henry, Cardinal York

SIGNIFICANT DATES IN SCOTTISH HISTORY

84	Calgacus and his men check Roman invaders at Mons Graupius near Stirling.
397 (*about*)	St Ninian founded Church of Candida Casa (Whithorn), Galloway.
560 (*about*)	St Columba founded Monastery of Iona.
584 (*about*)	St Kentigern (Mungo) Bishop of Glasgow met St Columba.
1057–93	Malcolm III ruled over most of Scotland.
1070 (*about*)	Malcolm III and his wife, St Margaret, founded the Benedictine Abbey of Dunfermline.
1265	Duns Scotus born, one of world's eminent philosophers and theologians.
1266	Hebridean Islands come under the King of Scotland.
1297	Sir William Wallace, Guardian of Scotland, won battle of Stirling Bridge against the invading English.
1305	Execution of Wallace.
1306	Coronation of Bruce, King Robert I, King of Scots.
1314	Battle of Bannockburn. Scotland freed for ever from foreign foes.
1329	Death of King Robert the Bruce.
1371	Accession of Robert II, first King of the Stewart dynasty.
1411	St Andrews University founded by Bishop Wardlaw.
1453	Glasgow University founded by Bishop Turnbull.
1467	Orkney and Shetland Islands become part of Scotland.
1494	Aberdeen University founded by Bishop Elphinstone.
1541	King James V with the Pope's approval designated 'Defender of the Faith'.
1542–87	Mary Queen of Scots.
1582	Edinburgh University founded.
1603	King James VI of Scotland became James I of England first King of Great Britain and end of the 300 years' war between Scotland and England.
1658–1719	William Paterson. Chief founder in 1694 of the Bank of England.
1714	Death of Queen Anne, last Stewart to reign in the direct line.
1715	Jacobite Rising.
1719	Jacobite Rising.
1745	Jacobite Rising.
1723–90	Adam Smith. His book *The Wealth of Nations* published in 1776.
1728–92	Robert Adam. He built Culzean Castle in 1777.
1756–1823	Sir Henry Raeburn.
1759–96	Robert Burns.
1771–1832	Sir Walter Scott.
1788	Death of Prince Charles (Bonnie Prince Charlie).
1790	Death of Flora MacDonald.
1795–1881	Thomas Carlyle.
1807	Death of Henry Stuart, Cardinal, Duke of York, brother of Prince Charles Edward Stuart, and last male in the direct line of the Stuart dynasty.
1812	*Comet*, first steamship in Europe, sailed down the River Clyde.
1822	King George IV visited Edinburgh. First royal visit to Scotland since that of King Charles I in 1641.
1850–94	Robert Louis Stevenson.
1855	Balmoral Castle built.
1866–1937	Ramsay MacDonald.
1876	Benedictine Abbey, Fort Augustus, founded. Benedictine monks who had lived abroad since 1560 now had their own abbey in Scotland again.
1878	Restoration of Scottish Catholic hierarchy.
1900	Queen-Mother born of old Scots family of Lyon, Glamis, Forfar (fourteenth century).
1952	Accession to throne of Queen Elizabeth I of Scotland, II of England.
1968	Dr R. Sanderson, Moderator of the General Assembly of the Church of Scotland visited Fort Augustus Abbey and assisted at divine service.
1969	Cardinal Gordon J. Gray. First resident Scots cardinal since the death of Cardinal Beaton, 1546.
1972	1st International Clan Gathering and Ceilidh.